COUNTRY ROADS

Brompton

PHOTO CREDITS

First published in 1987 by
Brompton Books Corp.
15 Sherwood Place
Greenwich, CT 06830
USA

ISBN 0-86124-348-X

Printed in Hong Kong

Reprinted 1990

10 9 8 7 6 5 4 3 2 1

Pages 2–3: A school bus plies the well-worn road
near a typical farm in the verdant, rolling countryside
of Pennsylvania, which the Iroquois Indians called
the 'Land of the Endless Mountains.'

Below: Cows grazing on a hillside, against the misty
sky; this scene could be anywhere, but the locale is
California's Sonoma County.

Alabama Bureau of Tourism and Travel: 44–45
Alaska Division of Tourism: 154 (bottom), 156–157
Orville Andrews: 108, 142–143, 164–165, 166–167
  (left), 170–171, 172–173 (right), 178 (upper left),
  178–179 (right)
Arkansas Division of Tourism: 154 (lower left)
British Columbia Ministry of Tourism: 145
Canadian Office of Tourism
  Mike Beedel: 150–151, 152–153, 158–159 (right)
  Egon Bork: 130–131 (left), 144, 168–169 (left)
  Alan Carruthers: 10 (upper left), 10–11 (right)
  Andrew Danson: 19 (upper right)
  Drie/Meir: 12–13, 14–15 (right), 16, 21 (upper right),
    97, 154 (upper left), 158 (upper left), 162–163
  Allan Harvey: 137 (upper right)
  Bill McLeod: 17, 160
  Dilip Mehta: 161
  Bruce Paton: 14 (left), 147 (upper right)
  R Semeniuk: 154–155 (right)
  Pierre St Jaques: 32
  Diana Thorp: 18–19 (left)
Four-by-Five: 1, 2–3, 8–9, 22–23, 34–35, 36–37,
  42–43, 88–89, 106–107
Florida Department of Commerce, Division of
  Tourism: 48, 49, 50–51 (right)
Georgia Department of Industry and Trade: 46–47,
  52–53 (left), 62–63
C J Hadley: 108–109 (right)
Paul Horsted: 98–99, 192
Kentucky Department of Travel Development: 57
© Kerry Kirkland: 50 (upper left), 126 (upper left), 131
  (upper left)
Louisiana Office of Tourism, Department of Culture,
  Recreation and Tourism: 53 (upper right)
Massachusetts Division of Tourism: 25 (top and bottom
  right), 41 (upper right) 58 (upper left)
The Reverend M J McPike Collection: 132–133, 138
  (top left), 138–139

Michigan Travel Bureau: 7, 70–71, 74–75 (left), 76–77,
  80 (bottom), 84
Minnesota Office of Tourism: 72, 73, 79 (upper right)
Montana Travel Promotion: 122–123, 124–125 (left)
Michael Murphy (TTDA): 116–117, 120–121
Nevada Commission on Tourism: 110–111
New York State Commerce Department: 24–25 (left),
  26–27, 28 (upper left)
Oregon Travel Information Section: 146–147 (left)
Salt Lake Valley Convention and Visitors: 113
South Dakota Department of Tourism: 90–91, 92
  (upper left), 92–93, 96, 102–103 (left), 103 (upper
  right)
Tennessee Tourist Development: 54 (upper left), 54–55
  (right), 60 (upper left), 64, 65, 66, 67
Texas Tourist Agency: 118–119 (left)
  Richard Reynolds: 119 (upper right)
Utah Travel Council: 112
Vermont Development Department: 20–21 (left), 28–29
  (right), 30–31, 33, 38–39, 40–41
Virginia Division of Tourism: 56, 58 (upper left),
  58–59 (right), 60–61 (right), 68–69
Wisconsin Division of Tourism: 75 (upper right), 78–79
  (left), 80 (top), 81, 82–83, 85, 86–87
Larry Workman: 169 (upper right), 174–175
Wyoming Travel Commission: 94–95, 100, 101,
  104–105, 134, 135, 136–137 (left), 140–141, 148–149
© Bill Yenne: 4–5, 115, 125 (upper right), 126–127
  (right), 128, 129, 167 (upper right), 172 (upper right),
  176, 177, 178–179 (right), 180 (upper left), 180–181
  (right), 182–183, 184 (upper left), 184–185 (right),
  186–187, 188–189, 190, 191

Designed and Edited by Bill Yenne

Photographs selected by S L Mayer and Bill Yenne

Captioned by Timothy Jacobs

CONTENTS

INTRODUCTION

If you've ever found yourself walking down that long and lonesome road staring at the glow of the sun as it settles low over a small town nestled in the pines, on the bank of an old free-flowing river—then you may recall a time in your life when the words 'country road' caused a rising in your chest that made you want to return, and linger there. There is nothing so peaceful as a country road—one of those narrow thouroughfares that are delicately but indelibly etched on the landscape and the psyche of the nations of the North American continent.

This book that I am privileged to introduce is a wondrous treasury of those roads that time forgot, yet are timeless and which will outlast in our fond memories even the grandest superhighways. The great railroads and highways of North America may be the bands that hold the continent together, but country roads run deep into the very substance of these great lands. These are the two-lane blacktops and gravelled ruts that lead us nowhere and yet everywhere.

Like the end of an age, like a sunrise, that clear watercourse of memory winds its way along the canyons, past buttes and cacti that seem to hover there, in the high desert heat, their bases separated momentarily from the cares of the Earth. Stay awhile, then follow. . .

Somewhere in the Northwest, an Indian fisherman tends to his mussel traps, and it reminds me of the time I sat and listened to a seasoned and cheerful fisherman, as he mended his nets and spun out tales of terror and sheer joy—the legends of a lifetime on the sea—years ago, and thousands of miles past in my own journey.

I remember the welcome hiss of the big rig's air brakes at sunset as the weathered truck driver delivered me from a blistering hitch-hike across the Oklahoma hills. He knew—and told me so—that the essence of the country road is one in sameness with the soul of this, the greatest of all great lands.

Beside crashing waterfalls, in the stillness of midday on the bayou, atop the spectacular beauty of the sheer rock cliffs, I stood and marveled, somewhere in the heavenly reaches of this continent and the tiny road that took me there.

That twister I saw dancing beneath a black cloud from the shelter of a Kansas farmhouse—it was the same, somehow, as the biting winds I was glad to be out of when the blizzard hit, and found that shack in Alaska. Or that wonderful mansion, remnant of another time—the warm courtesy the master of the house showed me when I stopped for directions in Georgia. . . it made me think of home, that little house by the brook, where the weeds and flowers intertwined in loving casualness, thanks to the kindly ministrations of dad's increasing fondness for things that grow of their own accord, and things that grow because we want them to.

I can remember so many times during the autumns I spent in Michigan, when renewal of a youth's fragile spirit meant a long drive up the Huron River Valley—alone with my thoughts, alone with *my* country road.

Here it is, a compendium of fondness, a photo album of another time that is yours to live. You need only set out on that small, buckled thoroughfare that is somewhere in your neighborhood, just down the block; a pathway to the wind, the sunshine and the rain—that country road that is, actually, best not forgotten, as its cleansing meanders strip away all that obscures your way.

It may not have been the longest that I've travelled, but the country road that will remain the longest in my memory is that narrow two-rut lane to Grandma's house. That last time, her lilacs were still there, but all was strangely silent. The low picket fence nodded sagely in the breeze, its roots softening in the soil.

—*William Patrick Jennings*

At right: In a favorite landscape for Sunday tourists, autumn leaves bedeck a road in rural Michigan. The air, so pure and crisp, is an invisible partner to nature's vibrant change-of-season display.

THE NORTHEAST

SPRING

The Spring is here, the delicate-footed May,
   With its slight fingers full of leaves and flowers;
And with it comes a thirst to be away,
   Wasting in wood-paths its voluptuous hours;
A feeling that is like a sense of wings,
Restless to soar above these perishing things.

We pass out from the city's feverish hum,
   To find refreshment in the silent woods;
And nature, that is beautiful and dumb,
   Like a cool sleep upon the pulses broods;
Yet, even there, a restless thought will steal,
To teach the indolent heart it still must *feel*.

Strange, that the audible stillness of the noon,
   The waters tripping with their silver feet,
The turning to the light of leaves in June,
   And the light whisper as their edges meet:
Strange, that they fill not, with their tranquil tone,
The spirit, walking in their midst alone.

There's no contentment in a world like this,
   Save in forgetting the immortal dream;
We may not gaze upon the stars of bliss,
   That through the cloud-rifts radiantly stream;
Bird-like, the prisoned soul *will* lift its eye
And pine till it is hooded from the sky.

——*N P Willis*

Previous page: A two-lane blacktop wends through a postcard-perfect New England village. *Above:* The sun shines on this modern-day Anne of Green Gables as she walks among the daisies on Canada's Prince Edward Island. *Right:* In a classic composition, on Prince Edward Island, flower garden, farmhouse and outbuildings are framed by rows of crops *(foreground)* and the Atlantic Ocean beyond.

AN ANCIENT CHURCH

Its stony sides are mossy-green with age,
   And round them rest the molded sepulchers
   Of many sacrificing characters—
The sainted hero, patriot and sage.
Archaic tablets on the walls engage
   Our solemn contemplation, and refer
   With love to each departed worshiper
As having earned a higher heritage.

We feel an awesome presence in the room
   Not classified or clearly understood;
Then, wondering beside a marble tomb
   Why all must join the silent brotherhood,
We leave the atmosphere of sacred gloom
   To hold communion with the living good.

——Willis Hudspeth

Below: Winding near this country church—dignified, and endowed with Prince Edward Island's Atlantic sunlight—a rural road leads travellers to the awareness that spring is in the air, as a sunset overcast betrays the abundant water that is—especially at this location—everywhere.

ALL BUS
TOURS
PLEASE
REGISTER!

Information
DEEP SEA
FISHING
APPLY HERE

INFORMATION

DEEP SEA
FISHING
SPACE
AVAILABLE

CANNED
LOBSTER
& CANNED
FISH

from
ON THE OLD FARM

Far away on the dear old farm
Is a home with a lasting charm,
　　Old and gray;
Its roof with moss is covered
Where the waving branches hovered
　　Many a day.

How often has the dawning
Of a beautiful June morning,
　　Long ago,
At my window blushed while telling
Of the roses sweetly smelling,
　　Just below.

The beauty, like a blessing,
Of Nature, sweet, caressing,
　　Filled the air;
The woods and fields were glorious,
And summer reigned victorious
　　Everywhere.

In meadows sweet with haying
We, happy children playing,
　　Wandered free;
The birds sang gaily o'er us
While we would join the chorus,
　　Full of glee.

——*Benj F Brown*

How cheery are the
　Those lovers of th
Their hearts are like
　As bounding and
They whistle when th
　In circles round th
And sing when deep
　Ploughs onward to

What care the marin
　There's music in t
When wide the berth
　And leagues of ro
Let billows toss to m
　Or sink to chasms
The vessel stout will
　Nor reel beneath t

There
　In c
　Wh
In sile
The ti
　A n
　Has
Transl

It repr
　Wh
Their
　A st
The m
　Of t

Above: His own father a man of the sea, this dapper
those who would visit his 'home port'—North Rustic
those who have the wisdom to pause awhile and li
memory's treasure chest—and what stories he has to

Above:
Edward
Gaspé P

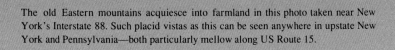

The old Eastern mountains acquiesce into farmland in this photo taken near New York's Interstate 88. Such placid vistas as this can be seen anywhere in upstate New York and Pennsylvania—both particularly mellow along US Route 15.

THE ROAD NOT TAKEN

Two roads diverged in a yellow wood,
And sorry I could not travel both
And be one traveler, long I stood
And looked down one as far as I could
To where it bent in the undergrowth;

Then took the other, as just as fair,
And having perhaps the better claim,
Because it was grassy and wanted wear;
Though as for that the passing there
Had worn them really about the same,

And both that morning equally lay
In leaves no step had trodden black.
Oh, I kept the first for another day!
Yet knowing how way leads on to way,
I doubted if I should ever come back.

I shall be telling this with a sigh
Somewhere ages and ages hence:
Two roads diverged in a wood, and I—
I took the one less traveled by,
And that has made all the difference.

—*Robert Frost*

Previous page: An antebellum mansion waits across the lawn as Miss Melanie comes to greet you 'by the roadside' in Alabama. *Below:* This classic Southern scene, posies in the foreground and porch-fronted grocery offering its shade, sings its gentle blues to the traveller in Pine Mountain, Georgia.

from

NATURE'S SONG OF GEORGIA

Down in sunny southland
Nature tells the story
Of its treasure store in Georgia
That is yet to claim great glory.

The wind goes whispering through the
trees
And bids them be content,
So good and greatly woods
Shall give the Nation recompense.

The sun and wind agree
That since ole Georgia has a share
In most of Nature's royal gifts
That they put all their climates there.

Georgia gives so many themes
For the birds to sing about;
Songsters stay the whole year through—
Then they never sing them out.

—*Vera McElveen*

OLD-FASHIONED LETTERS

Old-fashioned letters! How good they were!
    And nobody writes them now;
Never at all comes in the scrawl
On the written pages which told us all
The news of town and the folks we knew,
And what they had done or were going to do.
    It seems we've forgotten how
To spend an hour with our pen in hand
To write in the language we understand.

Old-fashioned letters we used to get
    And ponder each fond line o'er;
The glad words rolled like running gold,
As smoothly their tales of joy they told,
And our hearts beat fast with a keen delight
As we read the news they were pleased to write
    And gathered the love they bore.
But few of the letters that come to-day
Are penned to us in the old-time way.

Old-fashioned letters that told us all
    The tales of the far away;
Where they'd been and folks they'd seen;
And better than any fine magazine
Was the writing too, for it bore the style
Of a simple heart and a sunny smile,
    And was pure as the breath of May.
Some of them oft were damp with tears,
But those were the letters that lived for years.

Old-fashioned letters! How good they were!
    And, oh, how we watched the mails;
But nobody writes of the quaint delights
Of the sunny days and the merry nights
Or tells us the things that we yearn to know—
That art passed out with the long ago,
    And lost are the simple tales;
Yet we all would happier be, I think,
If we'd spend more time with our pen and ink.

——*Edgar Guest*

Above: Seeming to compose this very beautiful scene, which is truly 'visual poetry,' a cherry branch brings life to the folk phrase, 'Sweet Home Alabama.' *Right:* Ochopee, Florida boasts this, the smallest post office in the United States. They build things bigger in Mississippi—as is attested to by Eudora Welty's story, 'Why I live at the PO.'

CONTINUATION

Incessant tropic winds that pass
          Bestir the grass,
And whisper in the autumn calm
          The shepherd's psalm
Of life beyond the somber scene,
Where pasture fields are always green.

Nearby enduring blossoms shine
          From out a mine:
The ruby and the rhodolite
          Without a blight;
The purple, red and yellow quartz
That bloom for ages in the arts.

And, nearer still, a runlet sings
          Of hidden springs;
The constancy of their supply
          That falls from high.
Is't Immortality that speaks
This faith through zephyrs, rocks and creeks?

——Willis Hudspeth

Left: Tiger lilies give a distinctly Southern charm to this view of a Roswell, Georgia mansion. *Above:* The sun seems to rest among the limbs of this cypress tree, at day's end on Louisiana's Lake Palourde.

MY PAW SAID SO

Foxes can talk if you know how to listen,
    My Paw said so.
Owls have big eyes that sparkle an' glisten,
    My Paw said so.
Bears can turn flip-flaps an' climb ellum trees,
An' steal all the honey away from the bees,
An' they never mind winter becoz they don't freeze;
    My Paw said so.

Girls is a-scared of a snake, but boys ain't,
    My Paw said so.
They holler an' run; an' sometimes they faint,
    My Paw said so.
But boys would be 'shamed to be frightened that way
When all that the snake wants to do is to play;
You've got to believe every word that I say,
    My Paw said so.

Wolves ain't so bad if you treat 'em all right,
    My Paw said so.
They're as fond of a game as they are of a fight,
    My Paw said so.
An' all of the animals found in the wood
Ain't always ferocious. Most times they are good.

The trouble is mostly they're misunderstood,
    My Paw said so.
You can think what you like, but I stick to it when
    My Paw said so.
An' I'll keep right on sayin,' again an' again,
    My Paw said so.
Maybe foxes don't talk to such people as you,
An' bears never show you the tricks they can do,
But I know that the stories I'm tellin' are true,
    My Paw said so.

——*Edgar Guest*

Left: Through the falling leaves and over the fence, we see the village of Hightown, Virginia—on US Highway 250. *Above:* Kneeling in the autumn leaves, a father shares the wonders of the Kentucky landscape with his son. He remembers the time when, as a boy, he came to this same spot with his own father and heard the stories of their ancestors coming west with Daniel Boone to build a new life in these untamed, yet promising hills.

NATURE'S PLAY

Blue is the sky dome over the green,
Golden the sunshine sifting between
Branches that lazily sway in the breeze,
Showering the shadows under the trees
With arrows of light from the quiver of noon,
By the bow whose arch is the bright sky of June.

Sweet is the air with the perfume of flowers
Yielding their life through the long sunny hours;
With the song of the birds and the kiss of the dawn
To give them a welcome, their beauty was born.
And now seeks the sun its nightly repose,
While over its couch drapes a curtain of rose.

The clouds rolling upward in waves from the west,
Wear the colors of heaven with silvery crest,
Where the moon proudly sailing disperses her light
Till the little stars modestly creep out of sight.
These beautiful charms of the night and the day
Are glorious acts in Nature's grand play.

——*Benj F Brown*

Above: An Amish family takes a horsedrawn outing in the fertile Shenandoah Valley—both part of Virginia's wonderful heritage. *Right:* Cattle graze and flowers climb a fence in the lushness of southwestern Virginia.

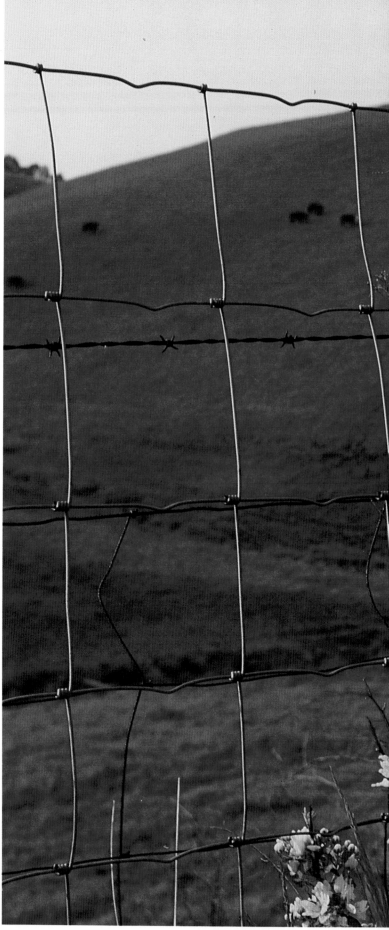

SOLITUDE

The ceaseless hum of men, the dusty streets
    Crowded with multitudinous life; the din
    Of toil and traffic, and the woe and sin,
The dweller in the populous city meets:
These have I left to seek the cool retreats
    Of the untrodden forest, where, in bowers
    Builded by Nature's hand, inlaid with flowers,
And roofed with ivy, on the mossy seats
    Reclining, I can while away the hours
In sweetest converse with old books, or give
My thoughts to God; or fancies fugitive
    Indulge, while over me their radiant showers
Of rarest blossoms the old trees shake down,
And thanks to Him my meditations crown!

——*William H Burleigh*

Left: A tidal stream winds its way amid the dunes to the Atlantic Ocean, on Georgia's Jekyll Island, near St Andrew's Sound.

LEAVING HOME

Within an ivied mountain porch a vase
    Is filled with bleeding hearts, o'er which is hung
    The portrait of a man when he was young—
A sabered scion of a fighting race.
A dog is peering in his master's face—
    That of an only son, who, called among
    His country's saviors, stands with stifled tongue
Before his mother in a fond embrace.

The mother's mother, fearing sacrifice,
    Looks strangely at the stars and stripes afloat;
To hide the moisture welling in his eyes,
    The waiting father turns to brush his coat,
While sister fumbles at her dress and tries
    To gulp the gorge arising in her throat.

——*Willis Hudspeth*

This old road *(left)* winds toward a Tennessee mountaintop under a canopy of brilliant autumn leaves—which in times past, and no doubt in 'times future,' has served to conceal many a 'white lightning' still, and has called many a country boy back home from the city.

Above: A tree bursts into fall foliage on this classic modern Tennessee homestead. The '57 Chevy reminds one of *Thunder Road*—the restless postwar youth of the fifties, homebuilt hotrods and a quiet country landscape that blazed with, and somehow encouraged, feats of untamed derring-do.

THE OLD LOG HOUSE THAT
GRANDPA BUILT

The old log house that grandpa built
Is standing where the fairies spilt
The seeds of peaches, tupelos,
Persimmons, firs and mistletoes.

The plaster lingers in the chinks;
Although the ridgepiece slightly sinks,
The cobbled chimney points as true
As in the days of sixty-two.

The absent attic boards reveal
The spokes in grandma's spinning wheel;
White clematis is vining still
Outside the kitchen window sill.

An iron pump is fastened where
The curving sweep and bucket were;
A platform with a mortared ledge
Supplants the soft and mossy edge.

Down by the river path is heard
Familiar musings of a bird,
And as I pass a honey hive
Endearing memories revive.

Meandering amid the glint,
I crush a stalk of peppermint
Declining in the garden yard,
And something makes me swallow hard.

Among the southern mansions which
Survive the ante-bellum rich,
Not one outvies, though trimmed with gilt,
The old log house that grandpa built.

———*Willis Hudspeth*

Above: Grandpa and his cronies enjoy a Veteran's Day celebration, Southern-style. Veterans all, they proudly salute the stars and stripes, although in his heart, Grandpa is still partial to the stars and bars.

Right: Grandpa's old house that has long since stood the test of time, weathers yet another southern autumn; getting set in its timbers once again for the chill and damp of winter.

THE GREAT

LAKES

from

MY NATIVE VILLAGE

There lies a village in a peaceful vale,
   With sloping hills and waving woods around,
Fenced from the blasts. There never ruder gale
   Bows the tall grass that covers all the ground;
And planted shrubs are there, and cherished
flowers,
And a bright verdure, born of gentler showers.

'Twas there my young existence was begun,
   My earliest sports were on its flowery green,
And often, when my schoolboy task was done,
   I climbed its hills to view the pleasant scene,
And stood and gazed till the sun's setting ray
Shone on the height, the sweetest of the day.

There, when that hour of mellow light was come,
   And mountain shadows cooled the ripened grain,
I watched the weary yeoman plodding home,
   In the lone path that winds across the plain,
To rest his limbs, and watch his child at play,
And tell him o'er the labours of the day.

And when the woods put on their autumn glow,
   And the bright sun came in among the trees,
And leaves were gathering in the glen below,
   Swept softly from the mountains by the breeze,
I wandered till the starlight on the stream
At length awoke me from my fairy dream.

Ah! happy days, too happy to return,
   Fled on the wings of youth's departed years,
A bitter lesson has been mine to learn,
   The truth of life, its labours, pains, and fears;
Yet does the memory of my boyhood stay,
A twilight of the brightness passed away.

My thoughts steal back to that sweet village still,
   Its flowers and peaceful shades before me rise;
The play-place, and the prospect from the hill,
   Its summer verdure, and autumnal dyes;
The present brings its storms; but, while they last,
I shelter me in the delightful past.

——*John H Bryant*

Previous spread: The Michigan shore of one of those great lakes which were once known as 'The Great Inland Seas.' *Above:* Like a village somewhere in Sweden, this pristine view of Center City, Minnesota seems to emanate fresh northern air.

Right: As this apple vendor of Swedish descent offers his wares, he actually appears to glow from within—or is it the small-town sunshine of Frontenac, Minnesota?

OCTOBER DAYS

In the golden haze of October days,
  In the woodland valleys and hills
There are showers of gold for the leaves grown old,
  Drop fast into Nature's tills.

Then the prickly burrs, when the sharp wind stirs
  Every branch of the chestnut tree,
Opened wide by frost, never heed the cost,
  But give of their treasures free.

O those woodland hills, how their beauty thrills,
  Bright tinted from red to gold;
'Tis a farewell song while we drift along
  Toward the days when the year is old.

——*Benj F Brown*

Left: A leaf-strewn two lane blacktop is a sign of impending winter—'mitten weather'—in the woods of rural Michigan. This old barn *(above)* affords an aged viewpoint for these very charming farm folk. Inadvertant windows and October's aromatic straw are but a few of the riches contained in the barns of Wisconsin, 'America's Dairyland.' *Overleaf:* Soon, with the winter's snows, some Michiganders will have to find another route to their favorite secluded spot, as the old dirt road is already in the depths of autumn.

from

AMERICAN WINTER

'Tis then the time from hoarding cribs to feed
The ox laborious, and the noble steed;
'Tis then the time to tend the bleating fold,
To strew with litter, and to fence from cold.
The cattle fed, the fuel piled within,
At setting day the blissful hours begin;
'Tis then, sole owner of his little cot,
The farmer feels his independent lot;
Hears, with the crackling blaze that lights the wall,
The voice of gladness and of nature call;
Beholds his children play, their mother smile,
And tastes with them the fruit of summer's toil.

From stormy heavens the mantling clouds unrolled,
The sky is bright, the air serenely cold.
The keen northwest, that heaps the drifted snows,
For months entire o'er frozen regions blows;
Man braves his blast; his gelid breath inhales,
And feels more vigorous as the frost prevails.

——*David Humphreys*

'The horse knows the way to carry the sleigh' sing these happy Wisconsin folks off on sleigh ride together *(left)*—an activity much favored during the long northern winter. There are much worse ways to spend a winter evening than 'snug and cozy' before the crackling fire of this Minnesota resort cabin *(above)*.

from
A HARVEST MASQUERADE

The passing menace of the clouds
revealed
A slender sickle in the starry field,
Illumining the fodder shocks that stood
Like Indian tents against the river wood.

Exploding softly in the early night,
A fountain dropped its jets of golden light,
And glittered only long enough to be
Transformed to meteoric nebulae.

This was the signal for a bursting shout
From young and older settlers starting out
In constellation dress and countenance
To decorate a neighbor's harvest dance.

The smiling pumpkins, lighted for the fete,
With gourd-made lanterns raised above the gate,
In keeping with the heavens, picturesque,
Shone forth a welcome equally grotesque.

——*Willis Hudspeth*

Left: These shocks of grain husks seem like monuments to the harvest—lit by the fading sun, watched over by the early moon. *Overleaf:* Like Abe Lincoln, this Illinois road follows the 'straight and narrow'—through the the winter landscape.

THE SOUTHWEST

A GRASSLAND F

Where buffaloes once pawed their pr
The loaded coaches of a train com
This picture of the great munificen
Of progress in the west which now p
The puffing locomotive almost fails:
The cars are wriggling up the emi
Jar forcibly the viaduct and fence
And lengthen out along the level rai

Deep drifts of snow have melted in
An iron windmill pumps a consta
But palpitates too speedily for one
Inclining to the vagrant while ag
Who, having climbed the red cabo
With places where he has to plov

—Wi

Previous page: This cattle drive along US R
ling of what 'life is about' in the Great Plain
couraging word, and the sky is not cloudy
farmer seems to think that his hard work is
slicker might be tempted to the difficult agri
as this *(right)*, with a yellow windmill rising

The
A b
Div

Old
An
Stil

The
An
Is l

Wh
Or
In s

Prev
mati
Abo
life,
ly il
hom

RAINBOW BRIDGE

A wide, precipitous and trackless wild,
   Impassable by vehicle or ass,
    Where rocks, rocks, rocks are jungled in a mass;
Rocks—massive, little, scattered, leaning, piled;
Rocks—dirty, splintered, rough and smoothly tiled,
   In thorny chaparral and rusty grass;
    Rocks—bright and clean, too different to class,
One-colored, mottled, striped, clear and riled.

Above this lonely gorgeous setting bows
   The famous red and yellow sandstone arc
Across a rapid rivulet that flows
   From Navaho and zigzags through the park.
When Nature built it not an Indian knows,
   And nowhere is an explicating mark.

——*Willis Hudspeth*

Only at one point in the continental United States do the boundary lines of four states—Utah, Colorado, New Mexico and Arizona—come together; the 'Four Corners' area, just a few miles west of Monument Valley, where these Navajo boys *(left)* shepherd their sheep.

Accessible by US Highway 163, Monument Valley Navajo Tribal Park is part of the extensive Navajo Indian Reservation, which extends into Utah and Arizona, and of course encompasses Monument Valley itself—scene of many a sensational sunset display of contrasts *(above)*.

THE MOUNTAIN

WEST

ODE OF A MOUNTAINEER

I think the city stores are grand,
  With polish, heat and fume;
But I am longing for the land
  Of sunshine, air and room.
The pines and canyons call me back
To life around my mountain shack.

I have enjoyed the limousines,
  Soft-cushioned, for a time;
But I am sighing for the scenes
  Where I shall have to climb,
Or hold fast in the old stage-hack
That jostles past my mountain shack.

I like the pavements, level, straight,
  Without a gulch or bluff;
But I am starting for the state
  Whose roads are steep and rough,
Up to whose jagged peaks a track
Leads winding from my mountain shack.

———*Willis Hudspeth*

Previous page: Going-to-the-Sun Highway in Glacier National Park leads us up toward the Continental Divide, in western Montana. Pack trips such as this one *(left)*—through Montana's beautiful, mountainous Pintler Peak country are always memorable occasions. *Above:* Spanning three generations of Montanans, an old cowboy poses with his granddaughter against a verdant backdrop.

from
LINES WRITTEN ON THE
ROCKY MOUNTAINS

These mountains, piercing the blue sky
   With their eternal cones of ice;
The torrents dashing from on high,
   O'er rock and crag and precipice;
Change not, but still remain as ever,
   Unwasting, deathless, and sublime,
And will remain while lightnings quiver,
   Or stars the hoary summits climb,
Or rolls the thunder-chariot of eternal Time.

It is not so with all—I change,
   And waste as with a living death,
Like one that hath become a strange,
   Unwelcome guest, and lingereth
Among the memories of the past,
   Where he is a forgotten name;
For Time hath greater power to blast
   The hopes, the feelings, and the fame,
To make the passions fierce, or their first
strength to tame.

Perhaps, when I have passed away,
   Like the sad echo of a dream,
There may be some one found to say
   A word that might like sorrow seem.
That I would have—one saddened tear,
   One kindly and regretting thought—
Grant me but that!—and even here,
   Here, in this lone, unpeopled spot,
To breathe away this life of pain, I murmur not.

——*Albert Pike*

Above: On its way to 'the sweet bye and bye,' a rainbow rises through the air over Cache Valley, Utah. *Right:* This is a view of Heaven's Peak, as seen from Going-to-the-Sun Highway, in Glacier National Park, Montana. If you step back a bit, and let your focus widen, you may be able to glimpse the gigantic halo surrounding the mountain.

THE HOME-TOWN

Some folks leave home for money
   And some leave home for fame,
Some seek skies always sunny,
   And some depart in shame.
I care not what the reason
   Men travel east or west,
Or what the month or season—
   The home-town is the best.

The home-town is the glad town
   Where something real abides;
'Tis not the money-mad town

That all its spirit hides.
Though strangers scoff and flout it
   And even jeer its name,
It has a charm about it
   No other town can claim.

The home-town skies seem bluer
   Than skies that stretch away.
The home-town friends seem truer
   And kinder through the day;
And whether glum or cheery
   Light-hearted or depressed,

Or struggle-fit or weary,
   I like the home-town best.

Let him who will, go wander
   To distant towns to live,
Of some things I am fonder
   Than all they have to give.
The gold of distant places
   Could not repay me quite
For those familiar faces
   That keep the home-town bright.

——*Edgar Guest*

Beyond the picturesque little town of West Glacier, Montana *(above)* is the west entrance of Glacier National Park, and the beginning of Going-to-the--Sun Highway, which connects at either end to US Route 2, and winds across the park.

Accessible by the Going-to-the-Sun Highway, Lake McDonald Lodge *(right)*, overlooking the lake, was originally part of a network of lodges built by the Great Northern Railroad as a spur to the development of tourism in Glacier National Park itself.

THE ROCKY ROUTE

The strait and narrow way is not
    A beaten path to gold.
It passes through a lonely spot
    Of failures manifold,
Most difficult to penetrate;
But, oh, the exercise is great!

You lovers of artistic deeps
    With eagerness to scout
And sketch among the rugged steeps,
    Look up the Rocky Route.
Upon a boulder you may land;
But, oh, the scenery is grand!

And all of you who want to teach
    The people what is best—
Especially you who would preach
    From individual test—
You may be sidetracked on this line;
But, oh, the inspiration's fine!

—*Willis Hudspeth*

Left: A young photographer prepares to truly take a 'closeup' shot of some mountain sheep near the ice fields on Columbia Mountain in west central Alberta. *Above:* Wildflowers bloom beside a hillside path in marvellous Glacier National Park, Montana.

Twisting, turning US Route 212 passes near Pilot Peak *(below)* in the Absaroka
Range of the Rocky Mountains. This rugged, handsome landscape lies a few miles
southeast of Cook City, Montana—just over the Wyoming border.

from
TOO HIGH

Where ridges rise up through the clouds,
And awe-inspiring art enshrouds
The master canyons' craggy walls;
Where gurgle white the waterfalls
From melting, ice-appareled peaks
To placid-running valley creeks,
I found a trail of recreation
That led to healthful meditation.

A marvel of the continent—
A Rocky Mountain monument—
Reflected vigor in each crest,
Associating thoughts of rest
With chiseled gardens of the gods,
Wherein the Sculptor threw the odds

And ends of grandeur that were left,
It seemed,
    When these great hills were cleft.

Its apex reaching to the sky,
A mighty summit towered nigh;
Secure, exalted and serene,
It pointed to the golden mean,
Directing undiscerning man
Up to the higher, wiser plan—
Up where, among the active spheres,
Fatigue in balance disappears.

Inspired by these environments
Of majesty and reverence,

I started up the steepest cone
That pinnacled the range—alone.
I followed in the ferny aisles,
Rewound around the sheer defiles,
And, after many hours of hope,
I tarried half way up the slope.

Jack-in-the-pulpits mutely preached
Of restfulness that may be reached
Around the lighted altar fires
Of sheltered tarns and granite spires,
Where, in the frankincense and myrrh
Exuding from the juniper,
The golden-vested songsters sing
Their sweet processionals of spring.

——*Willis Hudspeth*

Left: A pack string fords a stream near the base of Pendergraft Peak in Wyoming's Grand Teton National Park, near the Idaho border. In times past, these folks might have been miners prospecting for ore. These days, pack trains may be those of hunters or campers.

Above: This is a photograph of the Medicine Bow Peak area, part of the Eastern Rockies, in southeastern Wyoming. 'Medicine Bow,' like many other North (and South) American place names, is the invention of the area's original inhabitants—the various American Indian tribes.

FISHING

My grandfather said with a toss of his head,
    As he sat at the fire making flies,
Tying silk upon hooks for his old leather books
    And being mighty proud of his ties:
'Oh, the sport is a joy! But remember, my boy,
    Only hungry men work for the dish.
The creel's but a part of this glorious art;
    There is much more to fishing than fish.

'From spring unto fall I can answer the call
    To go out on my favorite streams,
And when wintry winds bite I can sit here at night,
    Enjoying my fancies and dreams.
For the soul can be stirred, both by blossom and bird,
    And the wonders that lie all about.
There are volumes of lore it's a joy to explore;
    Oh, there's much more to fishing than trout.

'It's not all in the catch; there's a thrill in the hatch,
    And knowing the birds by their song.
There's the tying of hooks and the reading of books,
    Which last a man all his life long;
Not a fisherman he who contented can be
    With the whirr of the reel and the swish
Of a taut running line, for the art is too fine!
    There is much more to fishing than fish.'

——*Edgar Guest*

Left: Pelican Creek, a fishing ground where many a 'big one' has 'managed to slip from the hook' after 'hours of battle,' winds toward the eastern boundary *(at rear)* of Yellowstone National Park, Wyoming. *Above:* This young angler has caught a trout—beginner's luck, no doubt—in Prince Albert National Park in central Saskatchewan, near Provincial Highway 2.

from

TOO HIGH

Above the elevated view
Was spread the bright celestial blue
That rolls the artist's eye and swells
His vision with ecstatic spells,
Till, dreaming in the tranquil breeze
And scenting balsam from the trees,
He loses in the arid haze
Off on the plains his ardent gaze.

Beyond a cabin by a pine,
Advancing to the timber line,
Where vegetation stunts and dies
And banks of snow increase in size,
I clambered through the wintry blast
Until the top was gained at last—
The farthest tip of earthly goal.
The scene disquieted my soul.

I saw the entrance of a chasm
Yawn wide as in a hunger spasm;
Down in the cold, abysmal black
I, cautious, peeped and startled back.

———*Willis Hudspeth*

Above: A traveller stands at the summit of Bear Tooth Pass, on US Highway 212 near the Montana/Wyoming border, in Custer National Forest. In the northern Great Plains states, one can stop the car almost anywhere, and just looking around, one can find a striking vista, such as that from Bear Tooth Pass *(right)*. Camping out on a shoreline always seems 'something extra,' especially in locales such as Cooks Lake *(overleaf)*, in Wyoming's Bridger Wilderness Area.

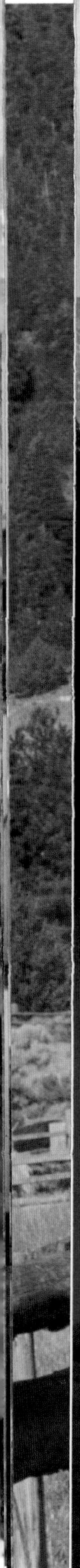

A MOUNTAIN

Beyond the grandeurs of the wide plateau,
　Against a Rocky Mountain's timber line,
　Surrounded by a frame of straggling pine,
A picture hangs in Colorado's show.
My pencils tipped with inspiration's glow,
　I try to reproduce the lucent shrine—
　The cleft, the granite boulders and the mine,
The mirrored zenith and the peak of snow.

I striv
　The
A lon
　My
And y
　The

Below: The beauties of a cloud-mottled day reflect in depthless Lake Tahoe. A dying tree catches the sunlight as if in farewell to its fellows, in shadow. The quiet and serenity evidenced here belies the extreme popularity of this—and the entire Sierra Nevada—area.

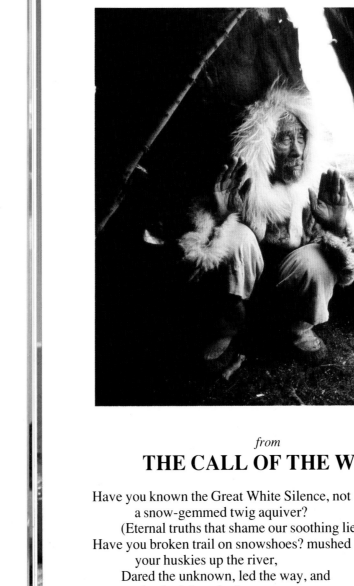

from
THE CALL OF THE WILD

Have you known the Great White Silence, not
    a snow-gemmed twig aquiver?
      (Eternal truths that shame our soothing lies.)
Have you broken trail on snowshoes? mushed
    your huskies up the river,
      Dared the unknown, led the way, and
      clutched the prize?
Have you marked the map's void spaces,
    mingled with the mongrel races,
      Felt the savage strength of brute in every thew?
And though grim as hell the worst is, can you
    round it off with curses?
      Then hearken to the Wild—it's wanting you.

Have you suffered, starved and triumphed,
    groveled down, yet grasped at glory,
      Grown bigger in the bigness of the whole?
'Done things' just for the doing, letting babblers
    tell the story,
      Seeing through the nice veneer the naked soul?
Have you seen God in His splendors, heard the
    text that nature renders?
      (You'll never hear it in the family pew.)
The simple things, the true things, the silent
    men who do things—
      Then listen to the Wild—it's calling you.

——*Robert Service*

A wizened Eskimo elder displays the lines of age and a lot of weather in this photo *(above),* taken near Alaska's Baker Lake, in the eastern continental Northwest Territories. The Eskimo call themselves Inuit, which is their word for 'The People.' Snowshoes, a dog sled and a sturdy tent *(right)* are essentials for winter travel in Canada's Northwest Territories.

Below: This Native Canadian, his skin tent pitched on the shore of Baker Lake in the Northwest Territories, has stood the test of tradition.

Above: Nuggets and flak
Creek, in Alaska's Yuko
loners who seek their 'ye

THE PACIFIC

COAST

A CYPRESS TREE

A wind-swept cypress tree of Monterey
Is leaning out to catch the ocean's spray;
One branch upraised, another sprawling low,
Are waving in the moon's resplendent glow.

Though but a photogravure of a scene
Presented in a nature magazine,
Some subtle charm, not sighted in the ken,
Impels one to reflect and look again.

——*Willis Hudspeth*

A Monterey cypress leans out from a northern California cliff in this photoportrait *(above)* of a sunset on the 'wide Pacific.'

Above: A man guides his small motorboat around fish traps set by the Quinault Indian tribe, on way his upstream at the mouth of the Quinault River in western Washington state. The spring rainclouds in the sunset are obviously dispersing, since 'red sky at night, sailor's delight.'

OLD CHURCHES

Hast been where the full-blossomed bay-tree is blowing
    With odours like Eden's around?
Hast seen where the broad-leaved palmetto is growing,
    And wild vines are fringing the ground?
Hast sat in the shade of catalpas, at noon,
    And ate the cool gourds of their clime;
Or slept where magnolias were screening the moon,
    And the mocking-bird sung her sweet rhyme?

Ay, pray on thy knees, that each old rural fane
    They have left to the bat and the mole,
May sound with the loud-pealing organ again,
    And the full swelling voice of the soul.
Peradventure, when next thou shalt journey thereby
    Even-bells shall ring out on the air,
And the dim-lighted windows reveal to thine eye
    The snowy-robed pastor at prayer.

——*Arthur Cleveland Coxe*

Above: This old, well-kept church is typical of the treasures one can find, 'just wandering around' the Pacific coastways. The Santa Barbara Church *(at right)* at Randsburg in southern California, is both a landmark and a place of worship.

from
A WHOLESOME SPOT

The weather, seventy degrees,
  With moisture at the happy mean,
Is smiling on a slope of trees
  Of citron, pea and balsam green.

Like boulders, clouds are piling high;
  A narrow gorge of paling blue
Is closing midway in the sky
  As yellow lightning filters through.

A soaring bird now turns and flaps,
  And in the scenery is heard,
With distant, softened thunder claps,
  The medley of a mocking bird.

The sweetest berries ever grown
  Are ripening and gone to waste,
And not a mountaineer has known
  An evil substance in their taste.

The tourist lingers to imbibe
  The wholesomeness that here abounds
And makes, which he cannot describe,
  A snakeless Eden of the grounds.

——*Willis Hudspeth*

Above: Coconut plantations in Hawaii made many an individual's fortune in bygone years. These days, they're mainly corporate affairs, or simply adornments for the state's country roads. *Right:* This rustic bungalow, with its garden and outbuildings, could be that 'little bit of paradise' that the careworn pilgrim has been seeking.

On the southern loop of Highway 11, the pleasant little village of Na'alehu *(below)*, on the island of Hawaii, claims the honor of being the southernmost village in the entire United States.

OUTWARD BOUND

The estuary surges with a raft
   Of ferry boats and liners, yachts and tugs,
   A man-of-war, floats crawling slow as slugs,
And fleets of various other masted craft.
Our hoarsely whistling steamer stirs abaft;
   The engine throbs; the vessel creaks, and lugs
   Its wedge-shaped prow around a pier, then chugs
A foaming fissure from its heavy draft.

                —*Willis Hudspeth*

Completed in 1936 during the halcyon days of WPA, this bridge *(below)* bears US Route 101 across the Yaquina River at Newport, Oregon—where the river meets the ocean, and the little boats set out upon the wide Pacific. US Route 101 'up the coast,' or US route 20 'over from Corvallis,' will get you there.

THE NEXT GENERATION

We shall leave you many problems; many tasks we
   couldn't do.
We shall leave a world unfinished that shall need the
   best of you,
And I wonder as I see you grouped in school and
   college still,
If you know the chance that waits you in the places
   you must fill.

The voice of opportunity is calling loud for men;
Men of wisdom, men of courage, to set right the
   world again;

Men of honor, men of vision; men the future's work
   to share;
And I wonder if you've heard it, and have started
   to prepare.

We have blundered; we have stumbled and have
   somehow lost our way.
In the wreckage of our failures we are gropers all
   today,
But you boys who follow after face a future strewn
   with need
And endless opportunities to conquer and succeed.

——*Edgar Guest*

Above: Californians in the summer of their youth scamper among the dunes, on a sunny Pacific coastal beach near California Highway 1—which follows the most extensive state coastline in the continental US. *Right:* As children through the ages have taken tentative steps along the road of life, these children walk hand in hand on a sun-dappled path in California's Big Basin State Park—dwarfed by the huge California redwoods, they are nonplussed but undaunted by the presence of such great age and size. In the light and shadow, their path along this country road is, for them, headed towards a bright future—'Happy Trails,' indeed.